BABY ANIMALS AND THEIR MOTHERS

A *terra magica* BOOK

HANNS REICH

Baby animals and their mothers

TEXT BY EUGEN SKASA-WEISS

HILL AND WANG · NEW YORK

People with a highly developed moral sense tend to give Nature a poor mark in humanitarianism. Nature is a heartless cannibal, they say, bringing forth new life–healthy, beautiful life–only to destroy it in the most ruthless way. Lavishly productive on the one hand, Nature is wantonly murderous on the other.

Yet moral and amoral people alike are unanimous in using the expression "Mother Nature." For, her cruelty notwithstanding, Nature does have a heart, a visibly beating heart: it is the great heart of motherhood. We must be broadminded enough to concede that the heart of the tigress and the hensparrow belong in that category, side by side with our own mother's heart. Maternity blurs the distinctions between human and animal life.

The sentimentalist can recall traditional animal characters: Bambi, the baby deer with the adorably rounded forehead, snuggling up to a supremely happy mother deer; a long-legged giraffe child, standing like a well-designed toy beneath the arching neck of its experienced mother; the lion cub, a truly cuddlesome, spoiled princeling, and his royal mother, who grooms him with a rough but tender tongue, her own personality transformed into a strange mixture of fierceness and the utmost in gentleness; the baby chimpanzee, all eyes and impertinence and terror, clinging to a loving, anxious mom. All have intensely human characteristics!

But let us abandon the human image for a moment and let us contemplate with respect and admiration the wolf spider's brand of mother love. The wolf spider ("lycosa" is its scientific name) is an eccentric creature. Its mores and philosophy are startlingly different from our own. Its maternal feelings, first of all, are concentrated on the sphere-shaped egg sac that contains its budding progeny. The arachnologist Crompton assures us that the female lycosa loves her cocoon more intensely than the most possessive human mother. The cocoon is the lycosa's be-all and end-all. She will fight for its safety with insane fury. Though we may detect no lovable features in it, the egg sac makes a different creature out of the lycosa. It may seem strange that mother love–that transcendent, selfless, self-sacrificing kind of love–should come into being here. Especially so, if we call to mind the lycosa's unfriendly habit of devouring her male partner immediately after the wedding night. Once having attained motherhood though, lycosa prefers death to living without her cocoon. If it is taken from her, she becomes demented. Her mind cannot tolerate a tragedy of such dimension. One cannot lose one's children; one does not give them up. Just as a cat whose kittens have been drowned will kidnap beaver cubs or even ducklings in order to lavish her bereaved affections on them, so one lycosa may occasionally steal another's cocoon as an outlet for her maternal love. There is yet a second act to this amazing mother love. As soon as the cocoon bursts open, two hundred microscopic spider babies climb up on their mother's patient back. She carries them along on all her hunting expeditions. If a section of the tiny passenger load drops off because the mother spider is overcrowded, she will stop and wait until every last one of her tiny infants has climbed back on. For six or seven months the baby lycosas live virtually on nothing but air. Their mother conscientiously shifts and turns at regular intervals so that every one of her darlings can get a sufficient dose of sunshine.

There are two important ways in which the prudent lycosa differs from, say, the human mother. In the first place, under her management, it is unthinkable that one of her babies could become a foundling. Secondly, she amazes us by the insouciant way in which she allows her young to move away once their time has come. She shares this carefree attitude with the vixen and the most motherly of hens, who is quite capable of taking an active part in the emancipatory process if her chicks insist on clinging to her beyond their allotted time. The wolf spider, who plans to marry again and is anxious to eat up a new husband so that afterwards she may again turn the full heat of her passion upon a new kindergarten full of eggs, goes even a step further than the pecking hen. Mother Nature has lent a warm maternal heart to the she-devil lycosa–but for a limited time only. Once that time is up, the old cannibal feels perfectly free to munch upon dawdling children who refuse to leave home. Let that be a lesson to them; only those who have sense enough to act at the right time will survive in life's struggle and strife. It's no use arguing with Mother Nature over such crass methods, for the history of spiderdom would long since have come to an end without them.

But, as if to prove that generalizations are nonsense, Nature has extended the burden-bearing patience of the mother koala bear across entire generations. The koala bear makes a much better behaved mother than the wolf spider, who does stick up so staunchly for her youngsters–up to a point. Koalas, those clownish marsupials, are found in Australia, the marsupials' native continent. The internationally beloved teddy bear is modeled after the koala mother and her cute, cuddly baby. As soon as the koala cub finds life in the maternal pouch too confining, he moves up on Mama's long-suffering back and clings there while mother climbs among the eucalyptus trees.

Mother Nature is particularly fond of clinging arrangements. For instance, she has been pleased to furnish the breasts of mother bats with special nipples to which the bat babies can cling while flying along with Mummy. Baby elephant shrews can find suction hold-on nipples even on their mother's shoulder blades. The field shrew, on the other hand, has another method. She teaches her little ones to form linked baby caravans and to walk in step with her wherever she goes. Burton reports on their nursery customs: "One of the babies fastens its teeth to the mother's back near the base of her tail, a second one attaches itself to the first one in exactly the same way, a third one fastens on to the second, and so on until the whole batch is arranged in a single straight line."

Some types of bats cling to the maternal chest in the same way as little capuchine monkeys do. To bring the spooky bat a little nearer to the human heart we offer a further comparison. Mother bats lick their newborn babies clean just as tenderly as mother cows and cats do. Of course, we must realize, as humans, that the word "tenderly" no more expresses the bat mother's true feelings than it conveys the maternal emotions of the cow, whose soulful gaze so impressed the Greeks that their greatest poet, Homer, did not hesitate to bestow the epithet of "cow-eyed" on Hera, the mother of gods.

Grzimek (a German naturalist) has observed a bat-like animal called the flying dog whose baby dropped from her breast when she was struck by a rifle shot. Though mortally wounded, the mother dove after her child and grasped it in mid-air before it could hit the ground.

No single-celled animal would dream of acting in a motherly or filial way. We know that Nature needed several million years to develop that controversial and character-transforming psychological drama we call mother love and place it, a specially precious offering, before the throne of God. Wasteful and inventive Nature could easily have devised some other means to safeguard life and its continuation. But she chose this highly emotional method of protecting her children against evil. She changes timid creatures who have entered into motherhood into flaming heroes who defy pain and death; she turns gluttons into ascetics, intolerance into patience, and egotism into self-sacrifice. She lends the tiny incubator bird the adaptable talents of a thermo-engineer and the tenacity of a construction worker. That little bird can move sixty-five cubic feet of sand and work itself into a state of exhaustion building a huge incubator for its eggs so that, in due time, a new incubator bird may continue that proud tradition.

Nature kindles the spark of maternal feeling in childless human godmothers and aunts and makes them unable to resist the animal baby's helplessness and charm. Human females are by no means the only creatures motivated by an urge that makes them stop beside every baby carriage and pick up and hug another woman's baby. Young elephants and giraffes enjoy the most lavish and loving attentions from maiden aunts–excellent, selfless mothers, even though the actual drama of motherhood may have passed them by. Bastian Schmid tells of a kindhearted hen that took any absent mother hen's chicks under her own wing at the sign of a storm. And Colette recounts a heart-rending story of a mother cat fighting off a strange black cat's competitive affection for her tom kitten Kamaralzaman. That black, would-be aunt was not a childless cat but, worse still, one of those unfortunates who had been robbed of her own children. In her bereavement, she offered her brimful nipples to the little tomcat in a secret way, and "her nostrils trembled like those of a human being fighting back tears."

This passion for stepmotherhood and aunthood inspires maternally minded rats with the absurd idea of adopting young mice instead of eating them up, as would be normal for a rat. Actually, the adopted mice deserve to be eaten, for they, in turn, mistake their tiny rat brothers and sisters for baby mice and vent their own pent-up mother instincts on them. This confusion of aunthood and adoptive motherhood can reach a point where a rat will carry a mouse in her mouth and the mouse, in turn, may carry a baby rat by the neck like a tiny doll.

In the dolphin family the ancient tradition of an aunt's loving care has more educational features. These intelligent, man-loving, legendary mammals give birth and nurse their young under water, as does the hippopotamus. As the moment draws near when a baby dolphin is about to be born–tail first and with a great deal of labor–a group of tense, excited, helpful females completely surrounds the mother. Like officious nurses they shoo away sharks and make the playful dolphin male understand that his presence is not welcome. The loving midwife, who is about to become an aunt, keeps herself ready to help the new mother with the baby's first swimming lesson and with the fatiguing job of guiding the newborn up to the surface for his breathing exercises in case the mother dolphin does not feel up to the task. The big-headed dauphins are taught to swim at the level of mother's dorsal fin and not to stray more than six feet from her side. In fact, they usually find themselves swimming between two female dorsal fins. The strict reins of this family education are somewhat relaxed after three months; it is followed by higher education in the ranks of dolphin schools. These institutions of higher learning are run as absolute matriarchies by groups of mothers and aunts. Needless to say, the youngsters don't always appreciate the advantages of such an arrangement. Their curiosity lures them, entices them away from the safety of the schools.

For, Mother Nature, who has equipped her mothers with special sets of instincts, has also implanted very definite drives and urges in the hearts of her children. Such a crossing of aims and purposes is bound to lead to conflict. Mother Nature has equipped the baby chick with an instinct to obey on the spot when the mother hen sounds a warning; but the more intelligent animal babies, who must serve a long apprenticeship in close contact with their mothers, are egged on by Nature to be unruly and naughty at an early stage. "Be curious, be nosey, in order that you may discover things on your own, for life will place you in situations in which mother's help will no longer be available!" whispers Nature to the restless young creatures. And they are torn between the need to satisfy their curiosity and the instinct for filial obedience. But the mothers, experienced and knowledgeable, bitterly disapprove of some of the things their youngsters think up; and the children—after a brief period of pretended docility—begin to protest irreverently against the continuous fussing and fretting because it begins to get on their nerves. The little kittens' tiny paws probe and poke in every corner and crack, and sometimes their thirst for exploration lands them with a plop in a bucketful of soapsuds. With luck they will soon know their way through the house. When their luck runs out, they may suddenly be heard meowing from the top of the roof, unable to get down without help. Puppies follow their sensitive noses into terrible, far-off places. The lanky camel youngster in the zoo refuses to understand why his mother insists that he react to a little springtime breeze as if it were a desert storm. She kicks him in the ribs to make him lie on the ground with outstretched neck and head, back turned to the wind, the way a proper camel is supposed to behave. But the young-ster is ungrateful and pig-headed; he resents being pushed around; sometimes his obstreperous behavior gets him kicked out of the family enclosure.

Mother dolphins, too, ask heaven to be their witness that their young are entirely too playful and high-spirited, entirely too carefree and teasing for their own good. But while sparrow mothers, for instance, have been observed to administer a sound thrashing to would-be runaways, the mother dolphin merely taps her babies cautiously on the nose, refraining from the crude method of a real thrashing. The young dolphin's teen-age pranks certainly displease and outrage his mother now and then. But what a charming, lovable prankster he is! People who have studied the customs and language of dol-phins are full of praise for the youngsters' delightful sense of humor and harmony. They manage to stir up the oldest of maiden aunts with their contagious high spirits and imagination.

Bear cubs, considered the acme in drollery by human observers, do not always get the same appreciation from their own adults. The bear mothers cuff them and smack them just as cat and hen mothers have cuffed and smacked their own offspring since time immemorial. Sometimes when a she-bear withdraws to a winter hideout in some cave or hollow tree, her cubs are born during that big sleep beneath the snow. They wake up beside a mother who is half asleep and who licks them drowsily. Some she-bears nurse their babies for two or three months without taking a single morsel of bark or berry themselves. The combination of doltish awkwardness and childlike grace that always delights us in a young animal is especially pronounced in bear toddlers. They are clumsy and playful, pugnacious, utterly childish, yet quick and athletic. In the Jämtland, in Sweden, a six-month-old bear was caught in a hailstorm. His poor little black nose was being bombarded by a thickening barrage of hailstones. Each time he was hit, he screamed in outrage, yelled for his mother, got up on his hind legs and tried to bat the nasty hailstones away with his paws. The harder it hailed the more furiously he fenced against the descending hailstones, until he stood completely engulfed by the dense stream of ice that kept falling all about him. What he did then shows how cleverly Mother Nature advises helpless young animals when they are far from their mothers, whispering excellent suggestions into their inexperienced ears: the little bear knelt down on his front paws, stuck his thick head down between them and resolutely presented his hindquarters to the hailstorm. In this classical attitude of provocative defiance he remained and waited stolidly until the hailstorm was over.

Her harsh educational methods notwithstanding, the mother bear loves her cuddly cubs with downright human affection: after all, it is not so easy to make something proper and presentable out of a bunch of willful buffoons when one's own blood runs red with earthy, buffoon-type willfulness!

Some baby elephants in the zoo have to be protected against the super-dimensional caresses of their mothers, whose maternal love clouds their huge heads to the point of danger. Even a doting elephant aunt can become a menace to the elephant baby. What a world of difference in the way animal children develop! The polar bear's infant does not trust himself to master the art of swimming without explicit instructions from his mother; the colt, however, no sooner arrives from his prenatal nirvana than the ancient horse sense takes possession of him: ninety minutes after his birth he trots after his mother; he knows without being taught that a smart horse takes care of unwelcome attentions by kicking out with his hind legs.

The half-open eyes of tiny predators snuggling against mother's protective breast have the same look of heavenly innocence as the eyes of the gentle lamb, the young antelope, the okapi, and the llama. Who would think of shrinking in terror from the "terrible lion" while holding a basketful of twelve-day-old spotted lion cubs in his arms? Their big childish heads dimly sense the approaching seriousness of life, and their soft little mouths give out faint whimpering noises because Mummy isn't there. I once saw a small black-and-white terrier bitch–she would have made a mere mouthful for a full-grown lion–lying in such a lion basket. The cubs were swarming all over her. Her own terrier pup sat among the yellow desert children, and they were being kind and brotherly to him and did not eat him. How had such a situation come about? Where was the mother lion?

The keeper explained that the lion's tongue had been too rough for her cubs. Each time she licked them they had screamed bloody murder. This had infuriated the lioness and she had boxed their ears. Finally, the chubby terrier bitch was engaged as their wet nurse. She brought her terrier pup along into the family. I saw her in a separate apartment of the lions' cage, loyal, lazy, alert, and immensely experienced in all questions of child rearing. "And what about the lion cubs' tongues?" I asked the keeper, seeing that the terrier nurse's nipples were bloody. "Can she stand their roughness?" "She puts up with that," was his reply; and it was true she did put up with it. "Also," he added, " being raised by a dog tempers the inbred wildness of the cubs." That last remark reminded me of a story by Ernest Thompson Seton in which upbringing had the opposite effect. In that story a human, a boy named Harry, became a snarling, biting menace after having been adopted and raised by a badger. Then there is, of course, Kipling's hero, Mowgli, who was stolen by wolves–the first wolf-boy of modern literature. The prototype of the she-wolf playing mother to humans–in whose lair the twins Romulus and Remus where prepared to go forth and found Rome–has been given a monument. And the Swedish naturalist Linnaeus earnestly records the cases of "ten such human animals," who were nursed and raised by wolves in sixteenth-, seventeenth-, and eighteenth-century Europe. The milk of their obliging savage nurses had made them rough and furtive, turned them into growling, meat-devouring Mowglies.

There is a basic affinity between children and animals. It is greatest when fearlessness goes hand in hand with curiosity, playfulness, and resourcefulness. Monkeys, elephants, dogs, and geese make the most reliable baby-sitters. Young monkeys have such a large repertory of games that they make excellent playmates for human children. Then again, there are the wild ducklings who have been raised inside an incubator without a mother. The first human being they see when they emerge from their incubator becomes a mother figure for them. They will follow their adopted mother around until they are fully grown.

In her moments of concern with budding life, Mother Nature has created an astonishing children's paradise, a place where every youngster is warmly received and cuddled and spoiled right down to the ground. This magnificent utopia for children exists in the sprawling subterranean residence of the prairie dog. There, any mother is ready to give her milk to any child who, in passing, knocks on her door and asks for a little nourishment. And since young prairie dogs are always on the go, nosey hedonists that they are, their appetite is simply enormous. Sometimes they even try their luck with male prairie dogs who happen to be lounging around the house. The males take these little mistakes in stride; instead of snapping at the erring babies, they turn their improper demands into fascinating games, hugging and caressing the little idiots into the bargain. No prairie dog mother ever resents a visit from someone else's child. Their love of children is so universal that they even admit teen-agers from neighboring communities who may have lost their way and entered the wrong burrow. With these outsiders, the mothers draw the line at bed and board, however. The strays must learn to obey the strict code of prairie dog ethics. They are given to understand that they can't stay. The mothers are firm about it. But they do not raise a fuss and hardly ever feel the need for calling in the male—the professional bouncer—to help get rid of the trespassers.

Storks have a much more stringent idea of family discipline. The male stork is a model father who combines strictness with gentleness. Flying lessons are a spartan affair; and woe betide the stork baby who forgets to hold his rear end daintily over the edge of the nest for purposes of digestion! Young storks who are being drilled in preparation for their first flight are wonderful to watch. But there is no coddling during these practice sessions, and each stork child has to pass certain tests of courage and endurance, as Theodor Lessing observed while watching a stork family's language-arts class in hissing and clacking. The father stork is not above taking a hand in the tasks of infant care. Sometimes he will stand for hours in the broiling sun to protect the little nestlings with his shadow. He also sprinkles them with water, which he brings from the pond in his crop.

Among the great father figures in the animal kingdom is the midas monkey. His habits are refreshingly different from those of the ne'er-do-well cannibal fathers we observe in other species. The midas monkey keeps his babies warm, warns them when danger approaches, defends them, and lets them ride on his back. One profoundly responsible father of the white-maned Liszt monkey family was seen slapping his wife's face because she was lax in her maternal duties.

In the strait-laced world of the stickleback the females are considered totally unsuited for maternal responsibilities. The male fish will not permit his varying harem of wives to help with the nest-building or child-rearing chores—a fact that does not seem to distress the girls in the least. They simply take off in a flurry of flirting fins. Mother Nature seems to have decided to make an example of the stickleback fish; to prove that if necessary, children can be securely and beautifully raised without a mother's help. For in this family the father has all the maternal instincts. He will not shrink from the wide-open maw of some predator about to swallow up a glassy batch of stickleback babies. He keeps the nest he has built as immaculately clean as an army barracks, airing it several times a day and herding would-be runaways back inside with a flip of his fin. He sees to it that the code of good stickleback manners is strictly adhered to by all his children.

It is, perhaps, cause for regret that seal fathers are by no means concerned over their wives' casual child-rearing methods. Extra babies are mercilessly disposed of, because seal families are firm believers in the one-child system. When an unwanted twin birth occurs, one unfortunate baby is left behind, to howl out its helpless heart on some deserted beach. The seal mother categorically refuses to rear more than one child at a time. Some of these poor deserted cry-babies have been rescued and sheltered and raised by human mothers. Later in life, these rescued seals have the greatest difficulty in overcoming their nightmarish memory of the vast ocean at whose shore they had been abandoned.

Karel Capek singles out the cat as an animal that simply overflows with maternal love—and who would not agree? A cat that has produced a basketful of kittens develops a kind of complete mother-fanaticism. The sight of a cat mother with her babies has inspired cat painters—such as Gottfried Mind and Karl Adam—to produce their finest pictures. A mother cat will hide her kittens when she suspects that some human being plans to do them harm. As for the tomcat—that untrustworthy, raffish creature—she evicts him from the nursery, spitting and hissing. But, there are exceptions. I had a Siamese cat once who produced two kittens. For a few days she was practically hysterical with pride in her enormous achievement. But after that she descended to the level of an ordinary tramp. She coldly refused to put up with all that mewling and crawling; the tiny creatures bored her. So she nursed them and then sauntered off, leaving them alone in their box. Presently, Papa Siamese stalked up to the box and climbed in–an ominous sight for anyone who knows tomcat behavior. But Reno, the tom, an old swashbuckler from way back, became a touchingly tender, affectionate father. He warmed the babies and licked them and purred over them. While his lady love lounged languorously in the garden, he taught the two kittens all the basic rules of cat caution and cleanliness. When they had grown their tiny masks, he introduced them to all important cat games, supervised their ritual boxing matches, and brought them mice. He demonstrated to his alert and fascinated students what must go before and what must follow the drama of the kill so that they could behave like proper cats once they caught a mouse of their own.

But the vagabond mother cat who prefers toms and human beings to her own kittens is the exception, not the rule. There are countless true stories about childless cats who have adopted baby mice, chicks, piglets, and newborn beavers, sheltering them, mothering them, and keeping them warm. One such stepmother cat even provided her adopted chicks–kidnaped from the chicken coop and carried to her own lair in the hayloft–with assorted greens to please their freakish taste. Cats have been known to lavish their maternal affections on baby hedgehogs and newborn land turtles. But the turtles are completely devoid of any kind of filial emotion, perhaps because they are hatched from eggs. There is the story of a cat in Lower Bavaria who was raising a young hedgehog as if he were her own. Desperately searching for her kittens, who had been drowned, this bereaved mother had come across a helpless bundle of quills with barely a breath left in it. The cat welcomed this opportunity to play mother to a young thing. She nursed the little hedgehog at her breast and gradually learned to beware of his quills. But every once in a while she was overcome by a need to groom that rough, spikey pelt. She licked it smooth. Sad and funny at the same time was

17

her despair at the fruitlessness of all her efforts. Those quills simply did not stay smoothed down. But, by and by, she accepted the idea that she had given birth to an oddball who did not even have the sense to comb himself. Mother and "son" sipped warm milk from the same dish and hunted for mice in beautiful family communion. Of course, the poor mother had a nasty shock the first time she saw her darling eat an apple.

The instinct of maternal love, the devotion of maiden aunts, and the impulse toward animal friendship are proof of the existence of something greater than man, in his arrogance, is willing to ascribe to that "lower" world: self-renouncing love. In its many forms this selfless love competes with the inbred instincts of self-preservation. For what is an empty stomach against a breaking heart?

Spendthrift Nature, so careless and cruel toward her children, has yet generously endowed many animals with the qualities of selfless love. Nature lets the fierce tigress become soft and gentle in the midst of her whining little balls of fur. The timid hen flies into a towering rage when any creature dares approach her while she is hatching her eggs. A perfect fury, she will land, squawking and beating her wings, on top of the bulldog's head. The tiny warbler mother flutters into the face of the marauding nuthatch and lures him away from her babies by pretending to be lame of wing or foot.

As children of human mothers whose maternal instincts have kept the human race going quite splendidly, we should not deny the title of mother love to the peculiar tenderness which animals show their young. Man is capable of surpassing any animal in cruelty. But the love displayed by both human and animal mothers has such divine features that even the least animal-loving of men will feel a supernatural thrill at the sight of a mother cat among her kittens. A breath of mystery from the kingdom of the Great Mother.

Translated by Maria Pelikan

PICTURE CAPTIONS

Front cover: Hedgehog. The female hedgehog produces an average litter of seven. *Erik Parbst*

Back cover: Horses near the lake of Neusiedel. *Herbert Seiler*

1. Mute swan. Both swan parents conscientiously protect their signets and defend them against all comers. *Rudi Herzog*

2. The chicken hawk, a bold adventurer, is indefatigable when it comes to providing his hungry chicks with a variety of choice morsels. *laenderpress*

3. Gray woodpecker. He loves a tasty mess of ants for himself and his offspring. *Walter Tilgner*

4. A walk in the woods is a rather unusual activity for a family of swans. The female swan lays up to nine eggs at a time and hatches them, all by herself, for five weeks. *Heinz Wedewardt*

5. This is not a real family idyl; the photographer merely decided to pose three frogs in this heart-warming group.
Rudolf Herbert Berger

6. Reed warbler. The young birds leave the protection of their nest when they are a mere twelve days old and have not yet quite learned to fly. But they are expert climbers even then, skillfully negotiating the reed wilderness. *Franz Pangerl*

7. Chimney swallow. The mother bird makes more than one thousand trips a day to feed her babies. She breeds as many as three times a year. *W. Wissenbach*

8. South American pampas ostriches with their two-day-old chicks. The chicks are hatched and raised by the father. With their powerful legs that can span more than twenty feet at a single step, ostriches are able to outrun even a horse. *Toni Angermayer*

9. Geese practice monogamy their whole life long. *Hanns Reich*

10. Twenty chicks—a record even for a duck. *laenderpress*

11. Porcupine. The porcupine babies are born with full vision and all their quills in working order. *Louisa Stoeckicht*

12. Water is the duck's own element. *Hanns Reich*

13. The llama is one of the world's oldest domestic animals. For thousands of years it has served as a source of wool and a means of transportation in the mountains of South America. *Gotthard Schuh*

14. The chamois is the only species of antelope existing in Europe. *Walther Rohdich-Bavaria*

15. The wood owl hunts at night. Its eyesight and hearing are extremely keen. *Erik Parbst*

16. The Australian koala bear is the living prototype of the teddy bear. *Garth Grant-Thomson*

17. Man's faithful servant, the horse, also makes an excellent mother. *Peter Thomann*

18. Boar pig. The sow produces a litter of up to twelve piglets every spring. *Niestlé-Bavaria*

19. The sloth is a vegetarian; its habitat is the South American jungle. *J. Bokma*

20./21. The three-horned chameleon changes its color according to its environment. Its color scale is particularly rich and varied. *Tobias Bjørn*

22. Tilapia Nilotica. The eggs are hatched in the fish's mouth. For some time after the little fish are born they flee back into the mother's mouth whenever they are in danger. *J. Bokma*

23. Sea lions are delightful to watch, both in the circus and in the zoo. *laenderpress*

24. Hippopotamuses attain a weight of more than twelve hundred pounds. Their babies are born under water and are nursed under water as well. *J. Bokma*

25. A polar bear born in captivity is a rare sight. *Black Star*

26. The dolphin is the most intelligent denizen of the sea. *Frank W. Lane*

27./28. Emperor penguins. Early in May the female lays a single egg which the male then hatches in a fold of his belly. While hatching, the male penguin goes without nourishment for ninety days. The young birds keep warm by sitting on their parents' feet. *Keystone, Lutetia*

29. Polar bear mothers have to be alert because the polar bear father frequently devours his own children. *Thomas Nielsen*

30. The brown bear takes her cub out of their den when he is ten weeks old, not before. *Paul Popper*

31./32. Polar bear cubs are small, helpless and blind for a long time. They are born no larger than rats. At the age of six months they are the size of dachshunds. Their mother takes care of them for years. *Black Star, UPI*

33. With tender caution the mother cat's sharp teeth grasp the kitten to move it to a safe place. *Archiv Braun*

34. The vulnerable newborn baby deer wears a protective dappled coat. *Wim K. Steffen*

35. Fallow deer. The baby prances daintily behind the alert mother. *A. Van*

36. The newborn lamb is kept warm by its woolly coat. *Keystone*

37. Hedgehogs are nocturnal animals. They sleep in the daytime, safe in their armor of quills. *Erik Parbst*

38. The goat is one of man's oldest domestic animals. *Rudi Herzog*

39. The aoudad lives in the sparse region of the Atlas Mountains. *Hanns Reich*

40. Young mountain sheep grow up in an austere setting. *Stefan Moses*

41. Every little pig has its favorite nipple. *Bon appétit! Bruno Kirchgraber-Lang*

42. Kangaroo kids grow up in the safety of their mother's pouch. Their natural habitat is Australia. *Tobias Bjørn*

43. For thousands of years the dromedary has been a loyal and frugal companion to the nomads in southern climes. *Rudi Herzog*

44. The opossum is a marsupial that can be found in the woods of the southeastern United States. On the ground it moves awkwardly, but up in the trees it is a great acrobat. *Roy Pinney*

45. Net-giraffe. The giraffe calf is five to six feet tall at birth. The mature animal is sixteen to eighteen feet high. *Tobias Bjørn*

46. A zebu cow washes her newborn calf. The Asian zebu has been used as a domestic animal as far back as 3000 B.C. *Toni Angermayer*

47. This lion cub feels perfectly at home with its father. *UPI*

48. See picture 45. *Emil Schulthess*

49. With the utmost delicacy the tigress holds the tiger cub in her teeth. *AP*

50. Seals are predators; they live on fish. On dry land they can only go places by sliding laboriously on their bellies. *Paul Popper*

51. Among thousands of zebras, no two wear identical stripes. *Emil Schulthess*

52. Gray baboons inhabit the coastal regions of Abyssinia and Arabia. They run in herds of from one hundred fifty to two hundred and forty animals. *T. Angermayer*

53./54. African elephant. The elephant baby remains a nursling for almost two years. It takes ten years for an elephant to grow up. *Emil Schulthess, Berretty-Rapho*

55. See picture 52. *UPI*

56. The hippopotamus is a total vegetarian. *Paul Popper*

57. The mother rhinoceros sniffs the air carefully, for the African steppe is full of dangers. *Emil Schulthess*

58. Gibbons are the most accomplished acrobats. To swing across a distance of thirteen feet is no problem at all for them. *Jost Camenzind-Collignon*

59. The mother orangutan shows her impressive teeth to frighten off

any would-be aggressor. *Newell Smith-Black Star*

60. It is easy for a mother baboon to hold on to her baby.
Heinz Müller-Brunke

61. The orang mother shampoos her baby with soft, tender lips.
Newell Smith-Black Star

62. Gorilla mother with her baby—a rare and triumphant event in a zoo. *Elsbeth Knöll-Siegrist*

63. A macaco mother with her nursling. *Tošo Dabac*

64. The orang baby can sleep peacefully while mother keeps watch.
Elsbeth Knöll-Siegrist

8

14

39

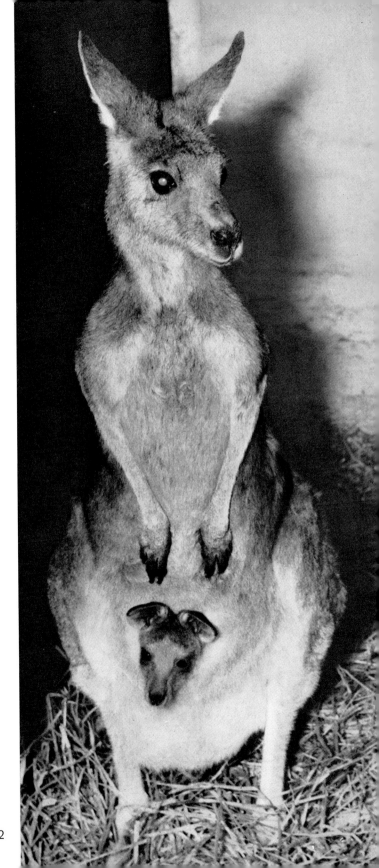

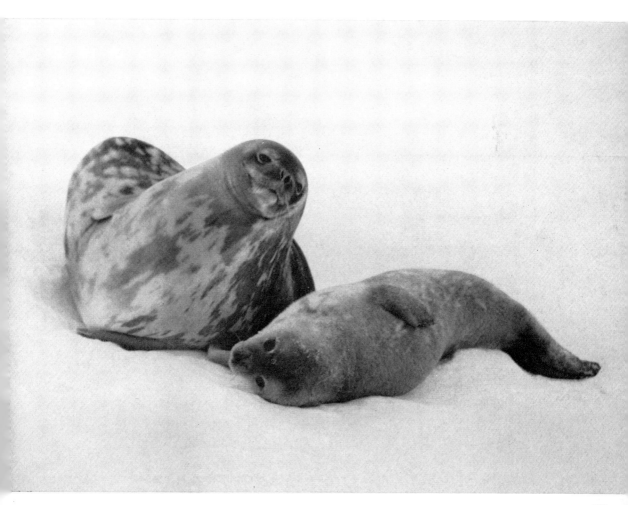